# MAKE YOUR MARK

# MAKE YOUR MARK

## CREATIVE IDEAS USING MARKERS, PAINT PENS, BLEACH PENS & MORE

LARK

**An Imprint of Sterling Publishing**
387 Park Avenue South
New York, NY 10016

Text © 2014 by Lark Books, an Imprint of Sterling Publishing Co., Inc
Photography © 2014 by Lark Books, an Imprint of Sterling Publishing Co., Inc
Photography page 6: upper left, upper right, middle right, bottom right,
page 12: top right, page 17 © 2014 by Maria M. Trujillo A.
Photography on page 6: top row middle, page 68 © 2014 by Amber Gameiro
Photography on page 11: bottom right, pages 13, 39, 40, 42, 44: bottom,
48, 49: bottom left © 2014 Dora Moreland

ISBN 978-1-4547-0846-9

Library of Congress Cataloging-in-Publication Data

Make your mark : creative ideas using markers, paint pens, bleach pens & more.
    pages cm
  Summary: "One look at Pinterest and the blogosphere and it's clear that crafters have embraced
markers as an easy way to add decorative elements to store-bought products. This primer showcases
30 wildly creative ideas for embellishing surfaces, including fabric, plastic, glass, wood, and stone.
Ranging from a batik tee to an oversized platter, the projects-and 100+ templates-were created by
crafting's top talents"-- Provided by publisher.
  ISBN 978-1-4547-0846-9 (pbk.)
  1.  Felt marker decoration.
  TT386.M35 2014
  745.4--dc23
                    2013030961

Distributed in Canada by Sterling Publishing
c/o Canadian Manda Group, 165 Dufferin Street
Toronto, Ontario, Canada M6K 3H6
Distributed in the United Kingdom by GMC Distribution Services
Castle Place, 166 High Street, Lewes, East Sussex, England BN7 1XU
Distributed in Australia by Capricorn Link (Australia) Pty. Ltd.
P.O. Box 704, Windsor, NSW 2756, Australia

For information about custom editions, special sales, and premium and corporate purchases, please contact
Sterling Special Sales at 800-805-5489 or specialsales@sterlingpublishing.com.

Email academic@larkbooks.com for information about desk and examination copies.
The complete policy can be found at larkcrafts.com.

Every effort has been made to ensure that all the information in this book is accurate. However, due to
differing conditions, tools, and individual skills, the publisher cannot be responsible for any injuries, losses,
and other damages that may result from the use of the information in this book.

Manufactured in China

2  4  6  8  10  9  7  5  3  1

larkcrafts.com

# contents

# introduction

With the ever-growing popularity of visually driven websites like Pinterest and Flickr, people are more inspired now to create their own DIY crafts than ever before. The value that creativity and ingenuity enjoy in our culture makes it even more rewarding. Never before in history have we been able to make a beautiful item, post a photo of it, and immediately have 15 people compliment it. And, of course, occasionally an idea goes viral—instead of 15 compliments, that beautiful, clever craft gets 15 thousand likes, shares, pins, and favorites.

Marker crafting is fun because it offers the opportunity to embellish our surroundings by beautifying everyday objects and upcycling old things that might otherwise find themselves in the landfill. It's an approachable craft— you don't need to know how to paint or even draw, and

you won't have to buy a bunch of paintbrushes and tubes of paint. In fact, very few supplies are needed. A marker, a surface to mark on, and your fertile imagination are all that's required to get started. Marker art is a portable craft that you can do anywhere—no studio needed!

*Make Your Mark* contains lots of eyecandy; it's a great source of creative fodder. Use the included templates as-is, trace parts of them and embellish freehand, mix and match different designs, apply each idea to a different substrate, or take the techniques you learn here and create your own unique pin-, share-, or post-worthy crafts. The possibilities are endless! You can use ideas from this book to make your own gift wrap, home and garden décor, custom gifts, party decorations, one-of-a-kind jewelry and clothing…or just art for art's sake!

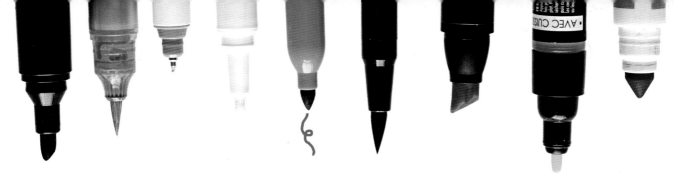

Marker crafting is simple and fun. You'll find that it doesn't require a big investment, has very few rules, and offers endless possibilities. Whether or not you're already a crafter or an artist, your imagination (plus a marker or two) is really the most important tool here. Now, let's commence sparking it!

# getting started

If you're a crafter, you might already have all of the needed supplies among your bins and boxes of craft things. The good news is that if you don't have them already, the list is short, and you won't need to spend a lot of money to get them.

## supply list

Most of the supplies you need for marker crafting can be found around the house. Cotton swabs, cotton balls, and a cloth rag are all handy ways of cleaning up mistakes. A rag is also a perfect fingerprint-wiper, and you'll always need paper towels for something. Rubbing alcohol should be on hand if you're using oil-based paint, and it isn't a bad idea to wipe off any non-porous surface with a rag and some rubbing alcohol before you even begin working. You'll need scissors to cut fabric and cut out templates if you opt to use them, and in some cases, to get that pesky marker packaging open! A few projects will be made easier by using a craft knife. A ruler will help you to draw straight lines as needed, and tape will come in handy for transferring templates. You will need a pencil for a number of things. Scrap pieces of paper or cardboard will allow you to press paint marker tips to get the paint out, test colors and designs, and wipe away blots that might occasionally appear on marker tips. Finally, of course, you'll need markers. You most likely already have a handful but before you begin any of the projects, you'll want to make sure you have the right marker for the job.

# markers

There are so many markers available, and it's wonderful to experiment with different ones on different surfaces, if that's your thing; but we've set out to make it easy for you to get started. We'll recommend markers we've tested and we know work well and ones that our featured artists love to use.

There are lots of ways to categorize markers: by the shape of their tips, by the surface for which they are made, by brand, or by the type of ink or paint inside of them. For our purposes here, we'll organize them by the latter—the medium inside the pen.

## paint markers

Paint markers come in a variety of paint types, but they all have a few things in common. A paint marker is essentially paint and a paintbrush in one. There is a chamber inside the shaft containing liquid paint that must be mixed (by shaking) before each use. There is usually a small ball or bead inside to help with the mixing, and you can hear it move around when you shake the pen.

Furthermore, most paint pens have a seal near the tip so the paint doesn't descend into the tip when the marker isn't in use, in order to keep the paint from drying out. Each different product will have its own instructions, but most will require you to press hard on the tip until it sinks into the end of the marker and wait for the paint to saturate the tip. The best place to do this, of course, is on a piece of scrap paper, or better yet, cardboard, so the paint doesn't seep through onto the surface underneath.

## oil-based paint markers

Sharpie and DecoColor™ Paint Markers are by far the most common products in this category, and they're available in a multitude of colors and tip sizes. You might see other brands in craft or office-supply stores, though, such as Uni® or U-Mark®. It seems worth mentioning that the DecoColor™ oil-paint markers also contain a solvent called Xylene. See the "Safety and Care" section on page 13 for more information on using Xylene markers.

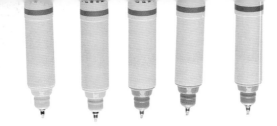

Oil-based paint markers are appropriate for almost any surface, and they're especially great for glass, ceramic, and other non-porous surfaces. The paint is opaque and water-resistant. That said, however, it isn't advisable to put an object painted with it through the dishwasher. In our tests, we've found it will survive on glass or ceramic for at least one cycle through the dishwasher if it's baked on, but why chance it?

If you make a mistake while you're working with oil-based paint markers, it's easy enough to wipe away any unwanted marks with a rag, cotton ball, or cotton swab (depending upon the size of the mark) and some rubbing alcohol. However, this wouldn't work well on porous surfaces like wood or fabric—only (most) non-porous ones like glass, ceramic, and sometimes terra cotta if you catch it soon enough.

## water-based (acrylic) paint markers

Acrylic markers used for projects in this book include Pebeo Porcelaine 150, Painters®, Sharpie® Water-Based, and Montana Acrylic. Other popular ones you might see are DecoColor™ Acrylic and Liquitex®.

You can use these markers on most surfaces, like you can the oil-based ones, but the paint isn't always as permanent, and it tends to be less opaque, though not always. Mistakes are even easier to clean up with water-based markers. On non-porous and even many porous surfaces, they'll easily wash away with water and a rag. Most acrylic paint will wash out of fabric in the washing machine, as long as it hasn't been heat-set in the dryer or with an iron. On wood, your success will depend upon how permeable the wood is, how prone the paint is to soaking in, and how dark the paint color is.

## ink markers

Ink-based markers do not usually require shaking or pressing the tip like paint markers do. Ink doesn't dry anywhere near as quickly as paint does, so it isn't necessary to keep it sealed inside the pen until you're ready to use it. Simply placing the cap on most ink pens and markers when you're done using them is protection enough.

Ink markers used in this book include: Sharpie® Permanent, Artline® Drawing, Prismacolor® Art Marker, Faber-Castell PITT®, ZIG Writer®, Prismacolor® Premier® Illustration, Copic® Sketch, Sakura® Gellyroll®, Sakura® Koi®, dip /calligraphy pens (which do not come with any ink inside, but rather you dip the tip into the ink of your choosing). The type of ink used varies from pen to pen. Some are alcohol-based, like the Sharpie® Permanent markers and Prismacolor® Art, and others will be waterbased. Some contain dye, while others contain pigment. The only difference of any consequence for our purposes is that alcohol-based markers dry more quickly than the others. Some markers are waterproof and others aren't, but you'll find that any product whose ink is waterproof will say so on the packaging.

As with oil-based paint markers, marks from most of these pens on non-porous surfaces can be removed using rubbing alcohol. This reaction can be used to creative effect too. For example, the combination of Sharpie® Permanent marker and rubbing alcohol on fabric creates a tie-dyed look. (See the projects on pages 38 and 44).

## specialty and craft markers

We've classified markers that are advertised for a specific function or feature as specialty or craft. While there is some overlap between this type of marker and the other two types we've discussed, craft and specialty markers are made with certain activities, surfaces, or effects in mind. The kind of paint or ink in these markers is of secondary or no importance. For example, the DecoColor™ Wood Stain marker is acrylic, or water-based, but it's made, packaged, and marketed as a wood-staining pen, not as an acrylic paint pen.

Specialty markers used in this book include the Clorox® bleach pen, Sharpie® Metallic permanent markers, and Sakura® Gellyroll®. There are scores of others available at craft stores, such as fabric, ceramic (including Pebeo Porcelaine), glass, terra cotta, and wood markers. How specialized are these markers, really? We've found that some of them work well on a variety of surfaces, like the DecoColor™ Terra Cotta, for example, while others truly make their best marks on the substrates for which they were made, like the aforementioned wood-staining pen.

Methods for removing marks and erasing errors made with specialty markers will vary according to the media. This can be difficult since some of the companies making these markers don't even print on their packaging or on their websites what base they've used. Try water first, and if that doesn't work, try rubbing alcohol, and finally, if rubbing alcohol doesn't work, try turpentine, start over, or get creative and cover up the error with a spontaneous design element!

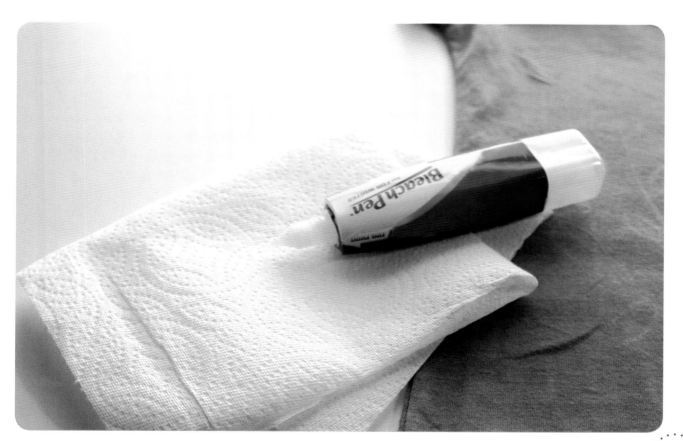

# substrates

Part of the joy of marker crafts, and what makes this book so fun to leaf through, is the incredible breadth of surfaces you can embellish with markers. In this book, we will present projects using various kinds of ceramic, fabric and canvas, glass, wood and cork, plastic, terra cotta, stone, paper, and cardboard.

The most important distinction among the various substrates is whether a surface is porous or non-porous. Porous surfaces, as you might have guessed, will soak up a lot of your medium. Fabric, paper, cardboard, and unfinished wood especially require markers that are on the wetter side: Sharpie® Oil-Based and other oil-paint markers, DecoColor™ Terra Cotta, DecoColor™ Craft Smart®, and surprisingly, Sharpie® Permanent are all wet enough to cover well on porous substrates, though the latter is not completely opaque on wood. On the other hand, non-porous surfaces call for pens whose media is on the drier side, like anything made specifically for glass or ceramic. The oil-paint and solvent-based markers do well on non-porous surfaces, too, though. Furthermore, brush-tip markers (markers whose tips are actually just like the end of a paintbrush) also seem to perform quite well on both types of surfaces.

## preparing the surface

No matter what kind of material you work with, it should always be very clean when you start working. Fabric, of course, is easy to clean—just wash and dry it according to the instructions on the label. Wood is a tough one. If you're working with unfinished wood, you will most likely not need to clean it, but it is a good idea to wipe or gently sand away any sawdust or burs, to ensure as smooth a surface as possible. If you are using reclaimed wood, you might choose to pressure wash it, unless of course the "dirty" look is something you want to preserve in your finished piece. In that case, just wipe the surface as clean as possible using a wet or dry rag.

Non-porous surfaces do require special attention. Of course you'll want to clean them with soap and water, but it's important to make sure there aren't any chips, cracks, or fingerprints. Chips or cracks in ceramic can cause the ink or paint from the marker to soak into exposed, unglazed parts and bleed in a way that's inconsistent with how it behaves on the glazed parts. Fingerprints, as trivial as they may seem, may likewise cause anomalies in paint or ink distribution, so be careful how you handle non-porous items, and polish off any fingerprints you notice.

## SAFETY AND CARE:

To be on the safe side, always use markers and rubbing alcohol in a well-ventilated area. Oil-based and solvent-based markers (Xylene, for example) emit strong odors. Turn on a fan, open a window, or work outdoors to avoid inhaling harmful fumes, and be sure to read the products' warning labels, following any special instructions set out there. Children using markers or rubbing alcohol should always be supervised.

Most markers are not food-safe. A few are labeled as such, but we encourage you to use your best judgment in those cases. In general, however, designs that you paint or draw onto plates, cups, and other items that come into contact with food or beverages should be limited to areas that won't touch food or an unsuspecting tea-drinker's lips.

Just like anything else you create in your craft adventures, you will likely take pride in the marker crafts you make, so of course you'll want to take good care of them. Always gently hand-wash your marker projects in a way that is appropriate for the type of pen and substrate you used. For example, anything designed using a water-based marker should be dusted gently with a dry cloth, because water can damage the design. Oil-based marker crafts, on the other hand, can be cleaned using warm water and mild soap, but don't scrub them, and don't put them in the dishwasher. Fabrics can be machine-washed on the delicate cycle and dried in the dryer. If you're not sure, err on the side of caution to protect your beautiful art!

# our tests

We didn't test every marker out there, just the most popular and readily available ones. We took five different substrates and doodled on them with the seven markers that worked best on each. Rather than bore you with charts and results, we thought we'd just show you what these babies can do!

## recommendations

Which markers should you use? We've done a lot of our own tests, and of course our contributing artists have their favorites. We want to share our findings and their preferences with you in hopes of taking some of the guesswork out of shopping.

**wood**

**Above from left:** Sharpie® Water Based Paint, Marvy® Wood Stain, DecoColor™ Craft Smart, Sharpie® Oil, Elmer's® Painter, Sharpie® Permanent, Gold Brush Marker

**ceramic**

**Above from top left:** Garden Craft® Terra Cotta, Sharpie® Permanent, Sharpie® Permanent, DecoColor™ Craft Smart, Sharpie® Oil, Gold Brush Marker, Pebeo Vitrea 160, Elmer's® Painter

**paper**

Above from top left: Pebeo Porcelaine 150, DecoColor™ Craft Smart, Elmer's® Painter, Gold Brush Marker Sharpie® Permanent, Sharpie® Water Based Paint, Sharpie® Oil

**glass**

Above from top left: Sharpie® Oil, Deco® Art Glass, Gold Brush Marker, DecoColor™ Craft Smart Elmer's® Painter, Sharpie® Permanent, Pebeo Vitrea 160

**NOTE:**

For the fabric test, we sprayed the fabric with a clear enamel spray paint before drawing on it, in order to keep bleeding to a minimum. You'll see that some markers still bled, a look you may want to use creatively.

**fabric**

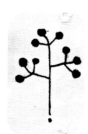     

Above from top left: Pebeo Porcelaine 150, Sharpie® Water Based Paint, Sharpie® Oil, Elmer's® Painter, Marvy® Fabric Marker, Gold Brush Marker

# artists' favorites

Each contributing artist told us which markers they used for their projects and, in some cases, the reasons for their preferences.

**Abbey Hendrickson**
Pebeo Porcelaine 150

**Amber Gameiro**
Clorox® Bleach Pen Gel

**April Deacon**
Sharpie® Water-Based, Extra Fine
Painters®, Fine (by Elmer's®)
DecoColor® Paint Marker, Fine
(oil-based)

**Dinara Mirtalipova**
DecoArt® Glass
Sharpie® Permanent, Extra Fine

**Dora Moreland**
Clorox® Bleach Pen Gel
Sharpie® Permanent

**Erin Inglis**
Prismacolor® Art Marker
Sharpie® Metallic
Sharpie® Oil-Based
Painters® (by Elmer's®)

**Esther Coombs**
Sharpie® Permanent
Pebeo Porcelaine 150

**Flora Chang**
Sakura IDenti®-pen
Sharpie® Oil-Based
ZIG® Writer
Faber-Castell PITT® Artist Pens
Montana Acrylic

**Note:** When she works on canvas, Flora likes to use the ZIG® Writer pen, but offers the following caution: "I tested a few red markers for this project and found that the red ZIG pen works the best with the black marker because it doesn't smear the black marker lines. Plus, it produces a bright red color. However, its red ink doesn't dry quickly on a canvas surface, so you must avoid touching the painted area. If you're right-handed, color your canvas from left to right and top to bottom. If you're left-handed, do the opposite. You can touch it without smearing once it's sealed with varnish."

Flora tells us that the Faber-Castell PITT® Artist Pens are the best pens she's tested for painting on unfinished wood surfaces, because they don't bleed.

When marking on top of acrylic paint, Flora prefers the Zebra pen because it doesn't bleed.

**Fusun Aydinlik**
Copic® Sketch
Sakura® Pigma® Micron®
Artline® Drawing
Prismacolor® Premier® Illustration
Sakura® Koi® Coloring Brush

**Ishtar Olivera Belart**
Sakura® Gellyroll® Moonlight®
Sakura® Gellyroll®Glaze®
Staedtler® Triplus® Fineliner
Pebeo Porcelaine 150

**Lena Hanzel**
Pebeo Porcelaine 150

**Maria Mercedes Trujillo A.**
Speedball® Hunt 512 nibs
Faber-Castell PITT® Artist
Pens, Brush
Copic® Multiliner SP 0.25
Sakura® Pigma® Micron®

**Ning Fathia**
Snowman® Permanent
Note: Ning uses Snowman acrylic paint markers, but you can't find those everywhere. In lieu of that, she says she finds that dry-erase markers work better on balloons than regular permanent markers. We found that other acrylic paint markers work great too.

# template and transfer techniques

We've included templates for many of the projects. Use them however you wish: enlarge them, reduce them, transfer all or part of a template, go freehand and use them as guides, or simply draw inspiration from them and create your own design. You can even mix and match templates, using pieces from multiple ones to guide you in creating a single design. Or use a template from one project on a different surface than what the artist has used. (Be sure to choose different markers as needed to accommodate different surfaces.)

The templates are made so you can transfer them directly to your substrate if you'd like to. Some objects, of course, have shapes that make this challenging, but most of the projects in this book feature surfaces that are flat enough to allow transfer. You might already have a preferred method for doing this, but if not, pencil transfer is a very easy method, and all you need is a copier, some paper, a pencil, and perhaps some tape.

Photocopy the template you want to use, and then trace over the ink on the front side of the photocopy using your pencil. Next, lay the paper, photocopy-side down, onto the surface you're decorating. Tape it down to keep it in place if needed, and then scribble over the back of the printed area with the pencil. When you lift the paper, you'll see a faint outline of the design, enough to see, but not so much it will show up in the final design.

## method for glass

Pencil transfer works great for most surfaces, except glass and fabric. Glass is easy, because you can see through it in most cases, so if you're decorating the outside of a jar, for example, you can usually just place the design inside the jar facing out and trace it through the glass.

## tracing paper for fabric

Fabric, on the other hand, requires a different work-around. The easiest technique we've found is using tracing paper and an iron-on transfer pencil. You just photocopy the template, enlarging or reversing it if necessary, trace the image onto tracing paper using a transfer pencil, flip the tracing paper pencil-side-down on the fabric, and iron it. This will transfer the pencil marks from the paper to the fabric, and they'll wash off in the washing machine later once you've finished your design.

# the projects

# chopsticks
designer **Flora Chang**

## what you'll need

- extra-fine tip acrylic paint markers
- pair of plain wooden chopsticks with four sides, lighter-color wood
- masking tape
- clear matte varnish spray

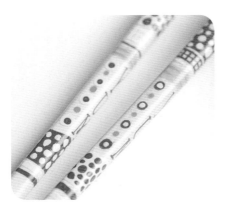

# what you do

**1** Using the acrylic-paint markers, start drawing your design at the thicker part of the chopsticks (the area where your food won't touch). Begin by drawing lines in alternate colors.

**NOTE:**
- Since the chopsticks' paintable surface is so small, it's better to paint simple patterns instead of complicated designs. (I did stripes, polka dots and some simple words on mine.) Also, I chose to paint each chopstick in reversing colors from one another to add interest.

**2** To make polka dots or stripes with a color background, start by coloring in the background area with one color, wait for it to completely dry, and then draw the polka dots or stripes on top of the background with a contrasting color.

**3** Continue working, mixing polka dots and stripes as you go, remembering to keep it simple. You can also add some food-related words if you wish.

**4** When you're done drawing, let the paint dry completely. Once the paint is thoroughly dry, wrap the unpainted part of the chopsticks with masking tape, leaving only the painted areas exposed. Spray a couple of coats of clear matte varnish to protect the painted areas.

**5** To clean your painted chopsticks, gently rinse them with water only.

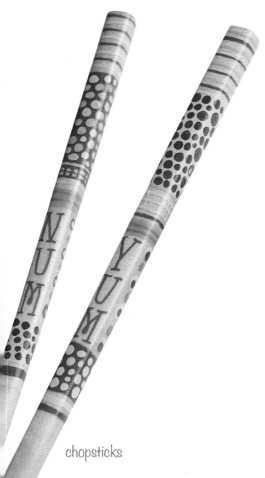

chopsticks

# cork coasters

## designer Flora Chang

### what you'll need

- desired number of round cork coasters, each 4 inches (10.2 cm) in diameter
- acrylic paintbrush
- acrylic paint in buttermilk color, or color of your choice
- template, page 24 (optional)
- brush pen, black (felt tip)
- clear matte spray varnish

### what you do

1. Load the acrylic brush with the color you'd like your coaster surface to be (I used an acrylic buttermilk color paint) and paint the entire coaster surface within the rim. (I kept the rim unpainted in order to show the contrasting color).

**NOTE:**
You don't have to use buttermilk paint for the background or black for the design. You can pick different colors, but make sure there is enough contrast between them so the design you draw will show up clearly.

2. After the paint is dry, transfer the template (optional), and use the brush pen to draw a design onto the painted surface. Pay attention to your line weight as you draw and adjust your pressure in order to achieve variations—this makes the design much more organic and interesting. Don't worry about trying to make it look perfect. You want it to look hand-painted and natural.

3. If you want to add interest to the rim, paint some bigger dots along it using the acrylic paint first, and then use the brush pen to draw smaller black dots on top of the buttermilk dots.

4. When you're done, spray a couple of coats of clear matte varnish on the painted areas to protect the finish.

# templates

templates are actual size

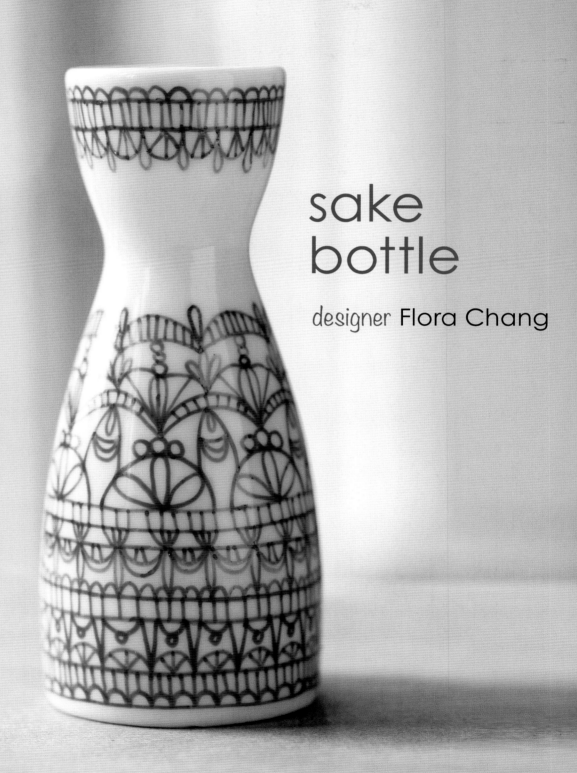

# sake bottle

designer Flora Chang

## what you'll need

- towel
- white porcelain sake bottle, 5 inches (12.7 cm) tall
- fine-point ceramic marker, blue
- template, below (optional)

# templates

repeat templates to make pattern

templates are actual size

## what you do

**1** Fold the towel and lay it on your working surface. It will serve as a cushion. Rest the bottom rim of the sake bottle on top of it as you draw, so the bottle doesn't slide around.

**2** Steady the bottle with your non-drawing hand, and lean it backward a little bit so it's on an angle. Using the template as a guide, start drawing with the fine-tip ceramic marker, rotating the bottle slowly and carefully as you draw.

**3** It takes practice to draw straight lines on a curved surface. Don't worry if you make an error, just wait for the paint to dry a bit, and then you can wipe it away with rubbing alcohol. Use cotton swabs for detailed areas and a paper towel or a rag for bigger areas. You can even wipe the whole bottle clean and start over! Don't let the rubbing alcohol touch any area you don't want to erase.

**4** When you're done, let the bottle sit for at least 24 hours so that the ink can dry completely.

**5** After 24 hours, follow the marker manufacturer's instructions for the proper heat setting in an oven. I baked my sake bottle for 30 minutes at 300°F (150°C).

# wedding signature plate

designer **Flora Chang**

## what you'll need

- large white porcelain dinner plate with a wide border
- extra-fine tip oil-based paint marker; red and black, or in two colors of your choice
- template, page 29 (optional)

## what you do

**NOTE:**

I used oil-paint markers in this case because their colors are solid, bright, and very opaque. They're not food safe and don't stand up well to frequent washing, but the plate is for decoration purposes only and won't need to be washed much. I find that the oil-paint markers actually draw more easily onto plates than porcelain markers do.

**1** Start by drawing or tracing the birds. Draw or trace the banner next, and then the lettering inside the banner. You'll use the black marker for each of these elements.

**2** Using the red marker, draw the heart between the birds, their cheeks, the flowers, and then the accents on the banner.

**3** For the border, alternate between the red and black markers. Draw the flowers in red and the stems and leaves in black. Do this until you fill the border all the way around the plate. You can go back to the red flowers once they've dried a bit and add some black dots inside the petals.

**4** If you make a mistake as you draw, simply use a cotton swab or a rag with some rubbing alcohol on it to clean up the error, and then continue.

**5** When you are done, let the paint dry and cure completely for a couple of hours. After that, the drawing should be pretty stable and won't come off unless you really try to scrape it off, or if you wash it a lot. If you wish, heat set the design by placing it in the oven for 35 minutes at 300°F (150°C).

A signature plate makes a great gift for any milestone occasion—to celebrate a birth or a 50th wedding anniversary. Friends and family can write their well-wishes, making it a memorable keepsake.

# template

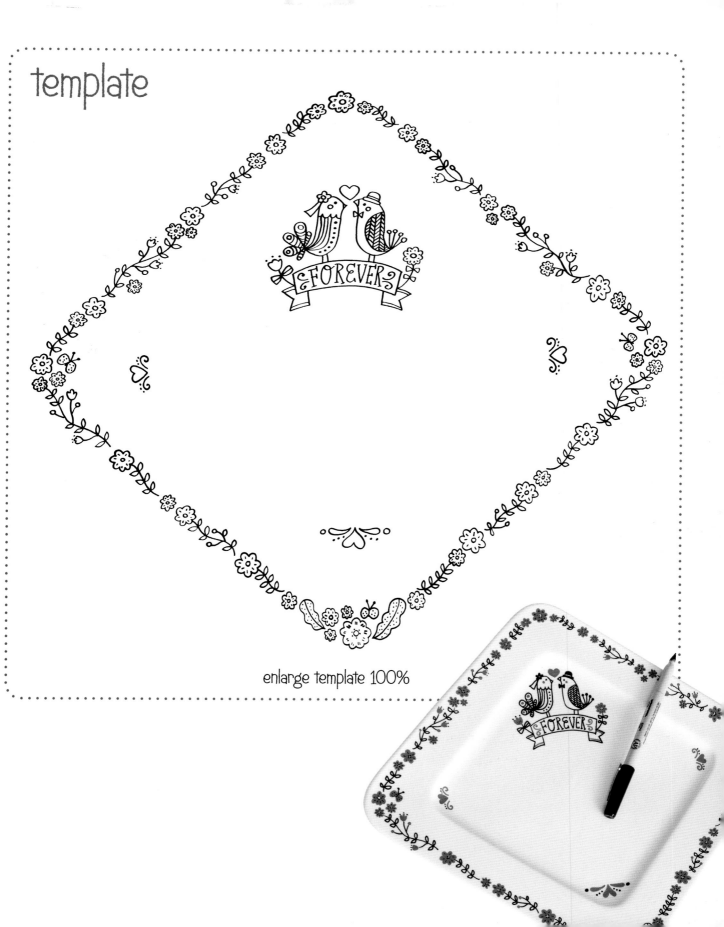

FOREVER

enlarge template 100%

# wooden knobs
designer **Flora Chang**

## what you'll need

- unpainted round wooden knobs, each 1½ inch (3.8 mm) in diameter
- pencil
- eraser
- circle template that includes 1-⅛ inch (3 mm) circles
- pyrography (wood-burning) tool equipped with its finest tip.
- pigmented India-ink artist pens with brush nibs
- clear matte varnish spray

**NOTE:**

- Be very light-handed when you sketch or transfer the design onto the wooden knobs using your pencil, and try to burn your lines following the pencil sketch as closely as you can. I've discovered that once the wood-burning tool makes its pass, the high heat "sets" the pencil marks into the wood and makes it really difficult to erase them later. So be careful. You can always test this on some scrap wood first and see if this is the case with your tool. Plus, it's always a good idea to practice your burning skills before you start.

## what you do

**NOTE:**

- Steps 1 and 2 are for people who'd like to do their own design with a circle border like mine, without using my templates. For people who will use my templates, transfer the templates (below) and start from Step 3.

**1** Using the pencil and a circle template, lightly draw a 1⅛ inch (2.9 cm) circle on the surface of the wooden knob. Try to make the circle as centered as possible. If you find it's not quite centered, erase it and try again. This will be the circle for the scallop border. At this point, you can sketch out the little scallops with your pencil, or just go freehand later with the wood-burning tool.

**2** Sketch your design within the circle. If you want to draw another circle within the bigger circle, simply repeat Step 1 (by picking a slightly smaller circle on the template).

**3** When you're done with your sketch or template transfer, use the wood-burning tool to burn in all the areas that are to be black in the final design, carefully following the sketch. (Notice that some of the darkest areas you see in my sample are burned with the tool instead of colored with a marker.)

**4** Color the design with the pigmented Inda-ink pens. I like to keep my designs simple by using limited colors, but you can pick whatever color combo you want.

**5** When you're done coloring, spray a couple of coats of matte varnish to protect the designs.

## templates

templates are actual size

# kitchen word canvas

## designer Flora Chang

### what you'll need

- Gesso (optional)
- 12 x 12-inch (30.5 x 30.5-cm) framed artist canvas (coated with white gesso and ready to paint)
- template, page 35 (optional)
- black permanent ink, dual-point pen, fine/extra-fine, OR a black oil-based paint marker
- marker, extra fine
- red writer pen with a 1.2 mm bullet tip
- white acrylic paint
- small paintbrush
- clear matte varnish spray

## what you do

**1** Coat the canvas in gesso if it didn't come that way and let it dry.

**2** If you're using the template, transfer it onto the canvas.

**3** Draw the scalloped border with the black marker. Do the straight-line part of the border first, all the way around the canvas, and then come back and draw the scallops.

**4** Start drawing your words and doodles within the bordered area using the same black marker. Don't worry about the finished layout at this point. Just draw away and fill the whole space with words and fun doodles. Do this until the entire space is filled in.

**5** After all of the areas in black are done, use the red writer pen to color the black lines. Once you fill in the red color in one area, avoid touching it so it doesn't smear. The goal is to have a balanced layout at the end, with evenly distributed black and red design elements.

**6** Once the piece is complete, let it dry for at least 24 hours. Check to make sure everything is dry by gently tapping marked areas to see if they're tacky. When you're sure it's dry, you can correct any smears or errors by painting over them using white acrylic paint and a small paintbrush. Let the canvas dry thoroughly.

**7** Spray several (five or six) coats of clear matte varnish all over the canvas to protect it.

Use this same project idea to make a cheery canvas for the holidays.

GRILL tea LUNCH
burger
Eat BARBEQUE salad TASTE
YUM
DRINK MENU SIZZLE
COFFEE NUM
NUM
Griddle sweet bread
HONEY BAKE CHEESE
SOUP cookie breakfast
SEA SALT SUGAR CAKE
Apple noodle
ICE CREAM DINNER
delicious
chili

# template

enlarge template 100%

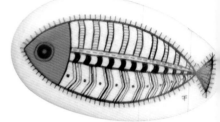

# painted stones

## designer Fusun Aydinlik

### what you'll need

- white pebbles with smooth surfaces*
- templates, below (optional)
- carbon paper (optional)
- pencil
- ink-based illustration marker, black, very fine tip (0.005 or 0.1)
- ink-based illustration markers in your choice of colors
  - black acrylic ink (optional)
  - 0 or 00 miniature brush (optional)
  - varnish (matte finish acrylic-based spray varnish or water-based deck varnish)

* stones must have a smooth surface; otherwise, fine lines may break or the ink may bleed

### what you do

**1** Soak the pebbles in soap and vinegar water for several hours or overnight. Vinegar will help kill the microorganisms in the stones' pores. Wash and let them dry.

**2** If you're using a template, trace it using carbon paper and a pencil. To get the template centered, make a hole in its geometrical center and try to place it over the geometrical center of your stone. If your stone is smaller or larger than the template, resize the pattern in a simple photo-editing program, or using a copy machine.

**3** Using the very fine black marker, draw over the marks from the template transfer.

**4** Paint the colored parts using colored markers. Try not to touch the black lines, because the black ink may mix with the colors.

**5** If desired, emphasize the pattern with thicker sizes of black markers or a paintbrush and acrylic ink.

**6** Seal the stone with varnish.

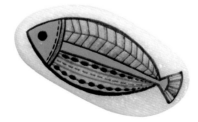

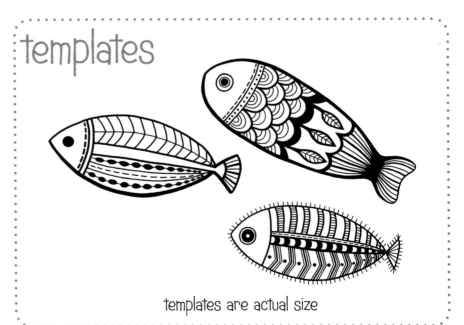

## templates

templates are actual size

# marker throw pillow

designer Dora Moreland

## what you'll need

- mist spray bottle
- rubbing alcohol
- white knit fabric
- cup or glass jar
- rubber band
- alcohol-based permanent marker
- iron
- embroidery thread
- embroidery needle
- desired color knit fabric
- needle and thread or a sewing machine
- fiberfill

**NOTE:**

- The ink really does its own thing for this project. Its beauty is in its abstractness and unpredictability. It's free-form, so have some fun with it!

This technique looks great on t-shirts, too!

# what you do

**1** Fill the spray bottle with rubbing alcohol. Adjust the setting to mist.

**2** Cut the white knit fabric to the desired size. Width and length should each be ½-inch (1.3 cm) longer than the actual dimensions you want your pillow to have, because the seam will take up ¼ inch (6 mm) on each end.

**3** Place the fabric over the mouth of the cup or jar and secure it with a rubber band.

**4** With the marker, make a dot in the middle and add 4 to 6 dots around it in a circle (photo a).

**5** Spray with rubbing alcohol and watch the color spread out and bleed in a circular pattern (photo b). Repeat the design with the jar in other places on the fabric.

**6** After the rubbing alcohol dries, iron the material with the highest heat recommended for the fabric, in order to set the color.

**7** If you'd like you can add a simple running stitch around some or all of the circles using embroidery thread.

**8** Cut the second piece of knit fabric (in your desired color) to the same size as the white knit fabric.

**9** Place the two pieces of fabric right-sides-together, and either with a sewing machine or by hand, stitch three of the four sides together. Turn the pillow right side out, fill it with fiberfill, and stitch the open side closed.

photo a

photo b

# bleach pen t-shirts

## designer Dora Moreland

### what you'll need

- iron
- freezer paper
- t-shirt,* prewashed and dried
- templates, page 43 (optional)
- white chalk
- transfer pencil (optional)
- hydrogen peroxide
- spray bottle or container big enough for submersing the shirt
- paper towels
- bleach gel pen

## what you do

**1** Preheat your iron on the highest setting.

**2** Cut a piece of freezer paper large enough to comfortably fit your design. Turn the shirt inside out and place the freezer paper shiny-side down on the shirt's (inside) front side. Iron the freezer paper onto the shirt as seen in photo a. Turn the shirt right-side out. The freezer paper will give structure to the fabric, and prevent the bleach from seeping through to the other side. If the freezer paper separates from the shirt, go over it with the iron again. No need to turn the shirt inside out again.

photo a

**3** Draw a design on the shirt with the chalk or transfer the template by tracing the design with a transfer pencil and ironing the design onto the fabric.

(See the instructions on the transfer pencil packaging.) A ruler can come in handy for measuring and drawing the lines if you decide to draw freehand.

**4** Prepare a mixture of hydrogen peroxide and water in the ratio of 1:10 (for example, 2 cups of hydrogen peroxide mixed into 20 cups of water) in a plastic container big enough to hold the shirt. The mixture should be a few inches deep in the container. If you prefer, you can fill a spray bottle with 1 part hydrogen peroxide and 5 parts water.

**Warning:** Please use caution when working with bleach products or hydrogen peroxide. Work in a well-ventilated area, and consider using plastic gloves, as hydrogen peroxide is a skin irritant.

**5** Grab paper towel and the bleach pen. Before you take the cap off, shake the pen a few times to make sure you get as much of the bleach gel to the tip as possible. You should repeat this each time after your draw a few lines to make sure you get an even flow to draw with. I always squeeze the pen a bit over the paper towel before I begin, to wipe away any air bubbles and to make sure I get a good flow going. I also do this each time I lift up the pen from the fabric. So keep the paper towel close by!

**6** Start tracing your chalk design with the bleach pen while gently squeezing it. Touch the tip of the bleach pen to the fabric very lightly and try to move at an even pace.

**7** When you're done tracing your design, wait a few minutes for the bleach gel to start discharging color. You can always lift up the shirt a bit to see the inside and peel away the freezer paper to see how the color is developing and to monitor how fast the gel is spreading.

**8** Hydrogen peroxide stops the bleach action, so when you're done, gently put your shirt into the container with the hydrogen peroxide and water without removing the freezer paper (see photo b). Do not fold or crumple the shirt; you want to keep the design as flat as possible so the bleach gel doesn't rub off onto unintended parts of the fabric. Slowly submerge the shirt into the solution and wait about 10 minutes. Gently rub off any remaining bleach gel from the shirt with your hand, remove the freezer paper from the inside of the shirt, and take the shirt to the sink to rinse it out.

If you're using the spray-bottle method, spray your design with the peroxide and water mix, making sure the bleach design is well soaked. Wait 10 minutes, and then rinse the shirt, washing away any remnants of the bleach gel. Wash the tee as you normally would.

photo b

If you have trouble finding t-shirts in a color you like, consider dyeing your own.

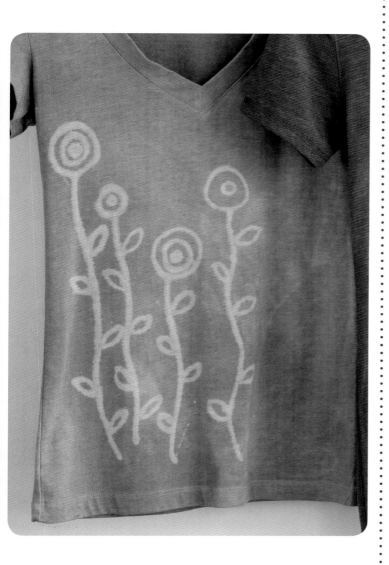

## templates

enlarge 300%

You can add additional details with fabric paint, simple hand stitching with embroidery floss, or beads and buttons.

# marker tie-dyed scarf

*designer* **Dora Moreland**

## what you'll need

- rubbing alcohol
- mist spray bottle
- alcohol-based permanent markers
- templates, page 46 (optional)
- silk scarf
- paper or cardboard
- old towel
- iron

**TIPS and TRICKS:**

● Before you start, test how the different marker colors will bleed on a scrap piece of fabric.

● Tilting the markers to the side a bit will produce thicker lines, which bleed much better than thin lines.

● Spray just a bit of the alcohol at first to observe how the colors spread. You can always spray more if needed.

## what you do

**1** Pour some rubbing alcohol into a spray bottle. Make sure it's a mist spray bottle or that it has a mist setting.

**2** Place the silk scarf on top of a piece of paper or cardboard and either draw your design freehand using the marker(s), or transfer the templates using a transfer pencil and an iron (photo a).

**3** Place the silk scarf on top of an old towel and spray the rubbing alcohol on the design. The rubbing alcohol dissolves the ink from the marker, which causes it to spread out or bleed, leaving a watercolor or tie-dye effect.

**4** After the rubbing alcohol dries, iron the scarf using the iron's "silk" setting to set the colors.

**5** Hand wash the scarf in cold water.

photo a

# templates

templates are actual size

# no-sew table runner

designer **Dora Moreland**

## what you'll need

- cotton or linen fabric, pre-washed and dried*
- iron
- freezer paper
- white chalk
- templates, page 50 (optional)
- bathtub filled with water or a spray bottle
- transfer pencil (optional)
- hydrogen peroxide
- bleach gel pen
- washing machine and dryer
- fusible webbing tape OR liquid seam sealant

* Table runners are not one-size-fits-all. You'll want to size yours according to your table. Your runner should be about ⅓ of your table's width, plus 1½ inch (3.8 cm) seam allowance (¾ inch [1.9 cm] on either side). The length should be the length of your table, plus 5 to 10 inches (12.7 to 25.4 cm) for overhanging on each side, plus the same seam allowance as for the width. I used a linen blend and incorporated the selvage edge into my design. It made for perfect, slightly fuzzy table-runner ends.

> You can add additional details with fabric paint or simple hand stitching using embroidery floss.

## what you do

**1** Cut your fabric a few inches larger than the desired size.

**2** Preheat the iron on the highest setting, and then iron the fabric.

**3** Cut a piece of freezer paper large enough for your design to fit comfortably. Place the freezer paper shiny-side-down on the wrong side of your fabric and iron it on (see photo a).

photo a

**4** Draw your design on the runner with the chalk or transfer a template by tracing the design with a transfer pencil and ironing the design onto the fabric. A ruler can come in handy for measuring and drawing the lines if you decide to draw freehand (photo b).

photo b

**5** Prepare a mixture of hydrogen peroxide and water in the ratio of 1:10 (for example, 2 cups of hydrogen peroxide mixed into 20 cups of water) in a bathtub. The mixture should be a few inches deep in the tub. If you're using the spray bottle method, mix one part peroxide and five parts water in a spray bottle.

**Warning:** Please use caution when working with bleach products or hydrogen peroxide. Work in a well-ventilated area, and consider using plastic gloves, as hydrogen peroxide is a skin irritant.

**6** Grab a paper towel and the bleach pen. Before you take the cap off, shake the pen a few times to make sure you get as much of the bleach gel to the tip as possible. You should repeat this each time you draw a few lines to make sure you get an even flow of gel. I always squeeze the pen a bit over the paper towel before I begin, to wipe away any air bubbles and to make sure I get a good flow going. I also do this each time I lift up the pen from the fabric. So keep the paper towel close by!

**7** Start tracing your chalk design with the bleach pen while gently squeezing it. Touch the tip of the bleach pen to the fabric very lightly and try to move at an even pace.

**8** When you're done tracing your design, wait a few minutes for the bleach gel to start discharging color. You can always lift up the shirt a bit to see the inside and peel away the freezer paper to see how the color is developing and to monitor how fast the gel is spreading.

**9** When you're done, gently put your runner into the tub with the hydrogen peroxide and water without removing the freezer paper (hydrogen peroxide stops the bleach). Do not fold or crumple the fabric; you want to keep the design as flat as possible so the bleach gel doesn't rub off onto unintended parts of the fabric. Fit as much of the runner as you can in the bathtub and submerge it into the solution. If some parts do not fit, soak it in sections. Gently rub off any remaining bleach gel with your hand, remove the freezer paper, and rinse the fabric out with clean water.

If you're using the spray-bottle method, spray your design with the peroxide and water mix, making sure the bleach design is well soaked. Wait 10 minutes and then rinse it out, rubbing away any remnants of the bleach gel. Wash and dry it as you normally would.

**10** Once the fabric is dry, iron it and cut away any long, loose strands. Since I like the frayed edges, I cut them even and simply applied a seam sealant along the edges to keep them from fraying more. You can also use fusible bonding web tape. To do this, first trim the edges to make them even. Then, with the table runner wrong-side facing up, fold ¼ inch (6.4 mm) over from the edge, and iron. Place the tape right in front of the ironed fold and make another fold (½ inch [1.3 cm]) to cover it (photo c). Iron the fold with a lot of steam. You can sew the seam to secure it, but it isn't necessary.

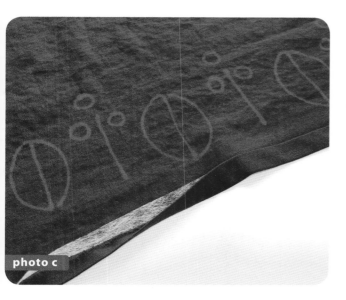

photo c

## HANDY TIPS:

● Head to the fabric store and pick out a few colors of fabric. At the cutting table, ask for swatches, which you can get for free or for less than a dollar each most of the time. At home, wash the swatches and test them with the bleach pen before you begin, to see how the bleach reacts with the fabric. Observe how fast the color discharges, and how fast the bleach spreads. Not all fabrics are the same. Some cotton fabrics or blends have been treated with a finish that does not react to bleach, or you may get a color you really don't like.

● The thickness or density of your fabric will determine how fast the bleach can spread. In a tighter knit, you will get more defined lines, but it may also take longer for the bleach to discharge color. In a looser-knit fabric, the bleach will spread much more quickly, and your lines will be less defined.

● Watch out for air bubbles in the bleach gel. Frequent shaking of the gel down to the tip will help prevent them and so will squeezing a bit of bleach gel out on a paper towel before you begin new lines. If you get a bubble at the end of your bleach pen's tip, simply wipe it away. If you keep marking with a bubble at the tip of the pen, the line you draw on the fabric might not appear solid.

● Practice, practice, practice. Grab old shirts, scrap fabric, or whatever you have lying around and practice drawing with the bleach pen. You should test out your design before you commit.

● If you're working on a larger surface, and you're concerned about some areas being exposed to the bleaching process longer than others, simply use the spray bottle with the hydrogen peroxide and water solution to stop the bleaching while you finish the rest of the design.

# templates

enlarge templates 300%

# doodle bowl, mug, and ornament

designer **Abbey Hendrickson**

To shake things up, try randomly filling in areas of your design or highlight a small section using a different color. You'll be surprised what a difference it makes!

## what you'll need

- white porcelain/ceramic bowl, mug, or ornament
- dish soap or rubbing alcohol
- ceramic paint marker, extra fine

**NOTE:**

- If you're making the ornament, be sure to remove its metal top before placing it in the oven. After the ornament has cooled, replace the top and attach the ribbon.

## what you do

**1** Use dish soap or rubbing alcohol to thoroughly clean the bowl, mug, or ornament. Allow the item to dry completely before you start to work.

**2** Use the paint marker to draw directly on the bowl, mug, or ornament, being careful not to smudge your marks. I prefer to work freehand, but you can also sketch your design on a piece of paper beforehand.

**TIP:**

- To create straight lines, stretch a rubber band around your object and trace just above it. Carefully remove the rubber band to continue drawing.

**3** Once you've completed your design, allow the paint to dry for 24 hours.

**4** Follow the manufacturer's instructions and bake the object to make the design permanent. Be sure to place the item in the oven before preheating it, and let it cool down in the oven for a few hours after you've shut it off.

# accented doily

## designer April Deacon

### what you'll need

- embroidery hoop
- doily
- acrylic clear coat
- acrylic or oil-paint pens in your choice of colors
- paintbrush
- decoupage medium

### what you do

**1** Center the most interesting part of the doily in the embroidery hoop and tighten the fabric until it's taut. Use care as you tighten it because doilies can tear easily.

**2** Spray the doily lightly with the acrylic clear coat. This will help prevent the paint pens from bleeding.

**3** Use the paint pens to highlight and embellish the existing designs on the doily.

**4** Trim the excess fabric to about ¼ to ½ inch (6 mm to 1.3 cm) outside of the embroidery hoop frame.

**5** With the hoop upside down, use the paintbrush to carefully brush decoupage medium onto the inside of the embroidery hoop and along the edge of the fabric. Tack down the edge of the doily as you go around the entire hoop until the loose fabric is completely glued to the inside of the hoop.

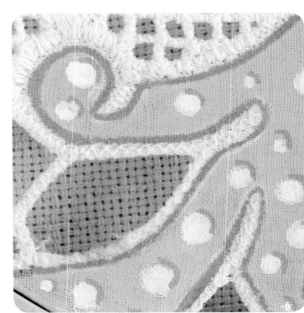

# repurposed tea towel

*designer* **April Deacon**

## what you'll need

- tea towel
- embroidery hoop
- acrylic clear coat
- fine-tipped acrylic- or oil-paint pens in your choice of colors
- paint brush
- decoupage medium

## what you do

**1** Center the most interesting part of the tea towel in the embroidery hoop and tighten the fabric until it is taut.

**TIP:**

- Marker crafting is a great way to upcycle or repurpose a dish towel that may be stained, because you can avoid using the stained areas or just paint over them.

**2** Spray the tea towel lightly with the acrylic clear coat to prevent the paint pens from bleeding.

**3** Sketch a design on paper. I sketched converging lines. They always seem to make things more exciting!

**4** Add your design to the tea towel using the paint pens. Your embellishments will relate better to the towel's original design if you continue with the same color palette.

**5** Trim the excess fabric to about ¼ to ½ inch (6 mm to 1.3 cm) outside of the embroidery hoop frame.

**6** With the hoop upside down, use the paint brush to carefully brush decoupage medium onto the inside of the embroidery hoop and along the edge of the fabric. Tack down the edge of the tea towel as you go around the entire hoop until the loose fabric is completely glued to the inside of the hoop.

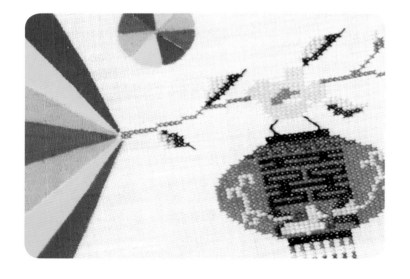

# upcycled handkerchief

## designer April Deacon

### what you'll need

- vintage handkerchief
- embroidery hoop
- acrylic clear coat
- acrylic- or oil-paint markers in your choice of colors
- paintbrush
- decoupage medium

## what you do

**1** Center the most interesting part of the handkerchief in the embroidery hoop and tighten the fabric until it is taut. I selected a hankie with a lace corner and an embroidered detail.

**2** Spray the fabric lightly with the acrylic clear coat, which will prevent the paint pens from bleeding.

**3** Sketch some designs on paper, choose the one you like best, and draw it on your handkerchief. I was inspired by the existing design on this hankie. I borrowed the leaf shape from the lace pattern and added shades of green.

**4** Paint your design on the handkerchief using the paint markers.

**5** Trim the excess fabric to about ¹/₄ to ¹/₂ inch (6 mm to 1.3 cm) outside of the embroidery hoop frame.

**6** Turn the embroidery hoop upside down and use the paintbrush to carefully brush decoupage medium onto the inside of the hoop and along the edge of the fabric. Tack down the edge of the fabric as you go around the entire hoop until all the loose fabric is completely glued to the inside of the hoop.

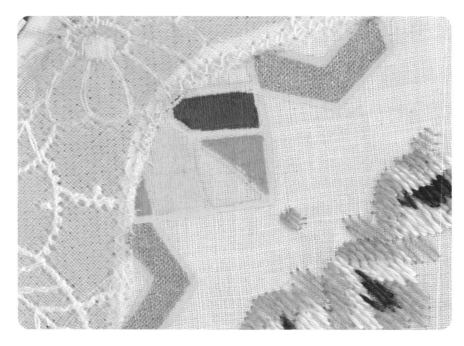

# adding text

designer **April Deacon**

## what you'll need

- photograph
- fine-tipped acrylic- or oil-paint pens in the colors of your choice

## what you do

**1** Select a photograph to embellish. You can find vintage photos in droves at antique stores, which is where I hunt for mine. You can also use family photos. If you're concerned about damaging the originals, simply have new prints made.

**2** Decide on the words you want to use. You may decide to repeat a single word or phrase. If the photo is of a family member consider writing significant facts about the person or something he or she often said.

**3** Find font samples. I like to browse online for interesting fonts to copy. For visual interest, I tend to mix up a few different styles.

**4** Write your words on the photo using the paint pens. While each photo is different, the background is often a good location to place words.

Talk about "putting words in someone's mouth!" Add the words to the photograph so that it looks like the subject is saying them.

# enhanced border

designer **April Deacon**

## what you'll need

- photograph
- fine-tipped water-based markers in the colors of your choice

## what you do

**1** Select a photograph. Try to get a photo with a plain edge or one that has been matted. Many antique photos are framed in beautiful mats, and it can be fun to add to an existing design.

**2** Practice a few designs or patterns on paper and then choose your favorite.

**3** Use the markers to draw or add to the border. I repeated the existing shapes in the border of my photograph.

# enlivened background

designer **April Deacon**

## what you'll need

- **photograph**
- **fine-tipped paint pens in the colors of your choice**

**TIP:**
- Water-based paint pens tend to have a matte, opaque finish, while solvent-based pens have a glossy finish.

## what you do

1. Select a photograph with a plain background.
2. Sketch some ideas for the background on paper. You could add a simple decoration like stripes or polka dots, or research traditional patterns from the time period when the photo was taken.
3. Draw your design on the photograph using the paint pens.

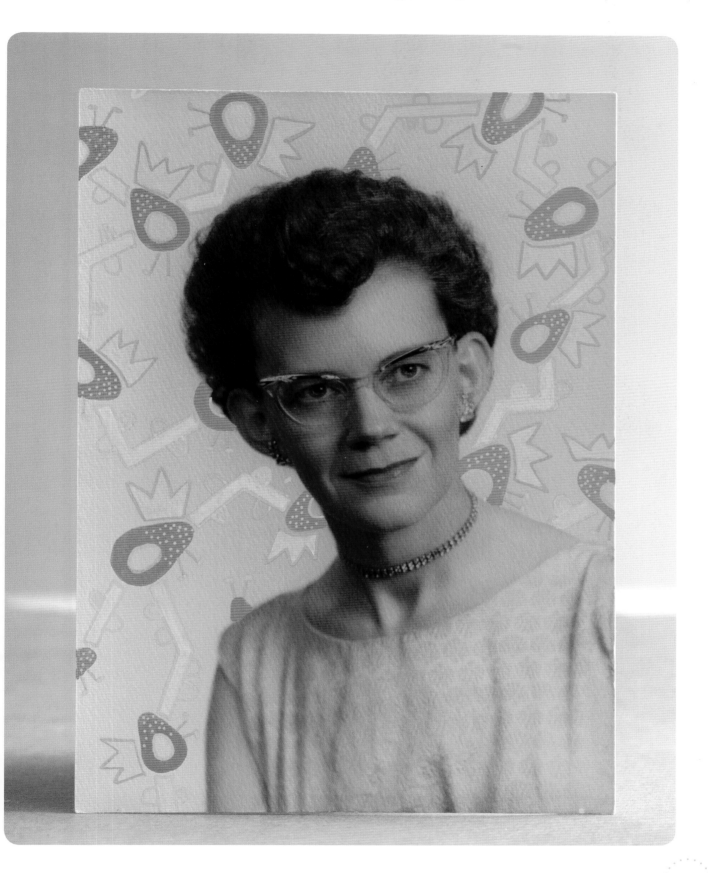

# new outfit

*designer* **April Deacon**

## what you'll need

- photograph
- water-based paint pens in the colors of your choice

## what you do

1 Select a photograph that includes a good deal of clothing in the frame.

2 Use the paint pens to add to existing patterns or create your own on the subject's clothing.

Try adding fun accessories like a hat or jewelry.

# pillowcase set

*designer* **Amber Gameiro**

## what you'll need

- iron
- pillowcase*
- white chalk
- transfer pencil (optional)
- tracing paper (optional)
- sheet of wax paper
- bleach gel pen
- washing machine

*Natural fibers like cotton, in dark or vibrant colors will yield the best results

## what you do

1. Wash and iron the pillowcase.

2. Sketch a design onto the pillowcase using white chalk (photo a). Keep the design simple.

3. Put a piece of wax paper inside the pillowcase to protect the back from any bleach that might seep through.

4. In a well-ventilated room or outdoors, trace the pattern you drew or transferred onto the pillowcase using the bleach pen.

5. Set the pillowcase aside in a safe place for 20-30 minutes, or until you like the color.

**TIP:**
- Make sure you use white chalk because colored chalk can stain the fabric.

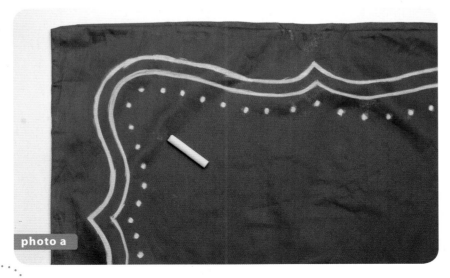

photo a

**6** Remove the wax paper lining and wash the pillowcase in cold water with detergent. Add the pillowcase to an already filled, agitating wash cycle (instead of putting it in and then filling the washer). This will decrease the chances of the bleach making contact with and bleeding to other parts of the pillowcase.

This technique is an attractive and easy way to dress up a plain throw pillow.

## what you'll need

- wooden birdhouse*
- acrylic paint
- paintbrush
- extra-fine tip permanent marker

* check your local craft store for a variety of plain wooden birdhouses.

## what you do

1. Using the project photo as a guide, paint a few circles with the acrylic paints on the birdhouse.
2. Use the marker to draw lines about an inch apart from one another.
3. Embellish the lines by drawing flowers and leaves.
4. To create more interest, doodle around the birdhouse's "front door," and add some details to the eaves.

You can go all out and doodle other fun details on your birdhouse, like windows with windowboxes and shrubs.

# templates

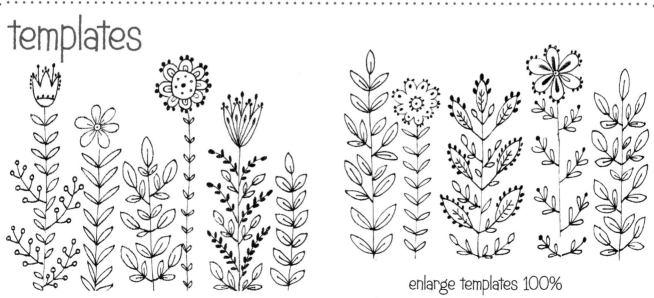

enlarge templates 100%

# glass cake-dome cover and bottles

*designer* **Dinara Mirtalipova**

## what you'll need

- **glass cake-dome cover**
- **templates, page 77** (optional)
- **glass-paint markers**

## what you do

**1** Clean the surface of the glass with a glass cleaner and allow it to dry.

**2** If you're using a template, simply place it inside the glass facing outward and trace the design on the outside using your marker. If you're drawing freehand, just begin doodling the design.

**3** Draw continuous, smooth lines without stopping. Any little imperfections can potentially be turned into decorative dots or flowers, but if you just don't like the way something looks, wipe it off with a paper towel and some rubbing alcohol.

**4** Draw the bold and main patterns first, and then add the decorative, intricate details to fill up the empty spots.

**5** Let your work dry, and then bake it according to the manufacturer's instructions.

Use these same instructions to draw designs on any decorative glass item (make sure the marker design doesn't come in contact with food). Recycled glass bottles and jars make pretty vases and storage containers.

# templates

templates are actual size

# gift box

designer **Dinara Mirtalipova**

## what you'll need

- coated cardboard box
- templates, page 80 (optional)
- extra-fine tip permanent marker

## what you do

**1** Get a box from a jewelry store or a local craft store. Boxes with a "coated" surface are best, as they accept the marker design easily and don't bleed.

**2** Start drawing your street scene. Draw simple square shapes, some taller, some shorter or wider, with a little bit of space in between them.

Dress up any white gift box with this cute design—no wrapping paper needed! The gift boxes that department stores give you work well. The cityscape looks great on coated cardboard envelopes, too.

3 Add the roofs, using a variety of simple triangle shapes. Remember, they don't have to be perfect. The quirkier, the better!

4 Add fun little details like windows, trees, flowers, and clouds, or anything else you desire.

5 Let your work dry completely before handling.

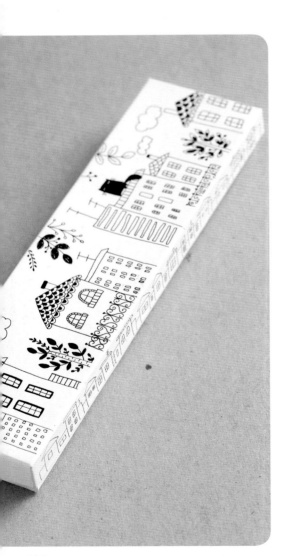

# templates

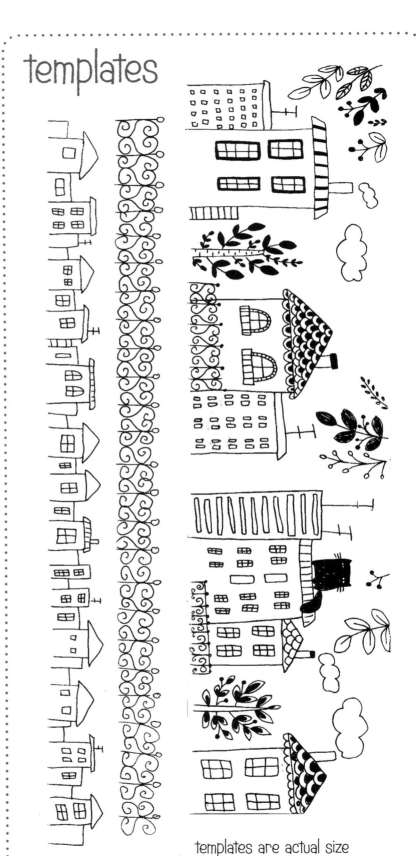

templates are actual size

# three-pane
# shadow box frame

designer **Dinara Mirtalipova**

## what you'll need

- **frame with multiple glass panes**
- **templates, page 83 (optional)**
- **solvent-based markers**

## what you do

**1** Clean the surface of the glass with a glass cleaner and let it dry.

**2** Play with your photo layout first. You may decide to place photos on multiple panes of glass. Once you're satisfied with your arrangement, firmly secure the photo/s with double-sided tape.

**3** If you're using a template, simply place it under the glass facing outward and trace the design on top of the glass using a marker. If you're drawing freehand, just begin creating the design.

**4** I suggest placing your design in the corners of the frame so it won't take away from the photo. To add dimension, draw the main part of a flower on the back pane and then add decorative elements to it on the front panes.

**5** Once the glass has dried for a few hours, gently wipe off any dust from the surface.

If you want to emphasize the multiple panes of glass, draw your design using different-colored markers for each sheet of glass.

# templates

enlarge templates 100% (each color represents templates on separate glass panes)

# all-purpose baggies

*designer* **Ning Fathia**

## what you'll need

- plastic bags, with or without built-in zipper seals, any size*
- templates, page 87 (optional)
- permanent marker, your choice of colors and tip width

\* the smaller the bags are, the smaller marker tip you'll want.

## what you do

1. Make sure your plastic bags are brand new, very clean, and free of fingerprints before you start drawing.
2. Place a plastic bag on top of the template you want to use.
3. Trace a design or draw freehand and let your creativity take charge!

Happy Birthday

Keepsakes from:
...........
When ... / ... / ...
Where .......................

this belongs to
Amelie

tea time

for you ...

OPEN
on
— / — / —

my first haircut
name : _____
date : _____

hello

JOSEPHIN

medicine

for a week.

made

# templates

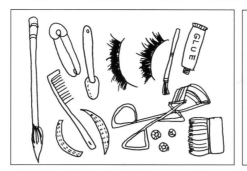

my first haircut

name : ...........................
date : ...........................

CLOTHESPINS

medicine

for a week.

hello

Bonjour!!

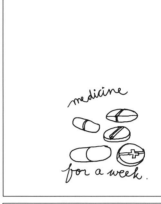

this belongs to

Amelie

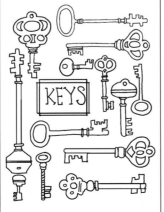

KEYS

JOSEPHIN

found at

..................

on

....../....../......

# celebration balloons

designer **Ning Fathia**

## what you'll need

- balloons*
- hand-operated balloon pump (optional) OR helium
- dry-erase markers

* when selecting balloons, look for the thickest and biggest ones you can find. Thick ones are less likely to pop, and big ones will display your designs better.

## what you do

1. Wash your hands before you start. The natural oils from your hands can interfere with the marker's ink, so the less you touch the balloons prior to drawing on them, the better. Make sure the balloon's surface is spotlessly clean. If the balloon has any residue or smudges on it, clean it with a rag and water, using soap if necessary.

2. Inflate the balloon using a pump (or sheer lung power) to a maximum of 80% capacity. If you blow it up bigger than that, it will be very easy to draw on, but it will be much more likely to pop! Once you've blown up the balloon, you can tie it right away if you intend to use it immediately. If you want to save it for later, hold the untied end tightly with your hand to keep the air inside.

3. Draw or write on the balloon, and let your creativity take charge. Be careful not to press too hard or smear the paint. Let your design dry. If you want to use the balloon immediately, and you've already tied it off, you're finished. If you need to deflate the balloon, proceed to the next step.

4. Let the air out, bit by bit. Do it slowly to keep from damaging your design. Even if you're sure that the marker's ink is dry, it may still smear, or worse, crack. If the design seems to crack or smear on its own, try using a different marker.

5. When you inflate the balloon the second time, I recommend filling it to less than 80%, and less than the first inflation is best.

These balloons make fun party invitations. Guests can read the deflated invitation and bring it to the party to inflate and celebrate!

# shrink plastic button set

designer **Erin Inglis**

## what you'll need

- sheet of white inkjet shrink plastic
- bullet-tipped art markers in colors of your choice
- circle templates or circle craft punches: 1½ inch and 2¼ inch (3.8 and 5.7 cm)*
- pencil
- scissors
- ⅛ inch (3 mm) hole punch
- parchment paper
- 320-grit sandpaper
- spray sealant

*Once shrunk, using the punch sizes above will yield buttons measuring approximately:
large: ⅞ inch (2.2 cm) in diameter
small: ¾ (1.9 cm) in diameter

**NOTE:**
- I use inkjet shrink plastic because it's pre-textured, which means it holds printer and marker ink well. Regular white shrink plastic would have to be sanded first for it to behave the same way.

## what you do

1. On one side of the shrink plastic sheet, draw a straight line from top to bottom using the widest part of the marker tip. Start with the blue marker and repeat with the other colors to form a large "rainbowed" section on your sheet.

2. Use the circle templates and a pencil to draw one large button and three smaller ones in the colored area of the shrink plastic, and then cut the circles out from the sheet. Alternatively, if you have the craft punches, you can punch out the circles without having to draw them first.

3. Add buttonholes to the circles using the hole punch.

4. Place the plastic rough side down on a piece of parchment paper to prevent sticking and shrink the plastic according to the manufacturer's directions.

5. Once everything is shrunk and cooled, smooth the edges with your sandpaper.

6. Cover the buttons with several thin coats of sealant until you have the desired shine.

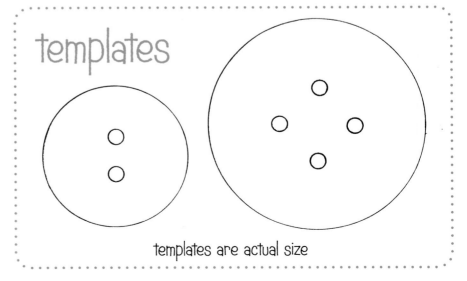

templates

templates are actual size

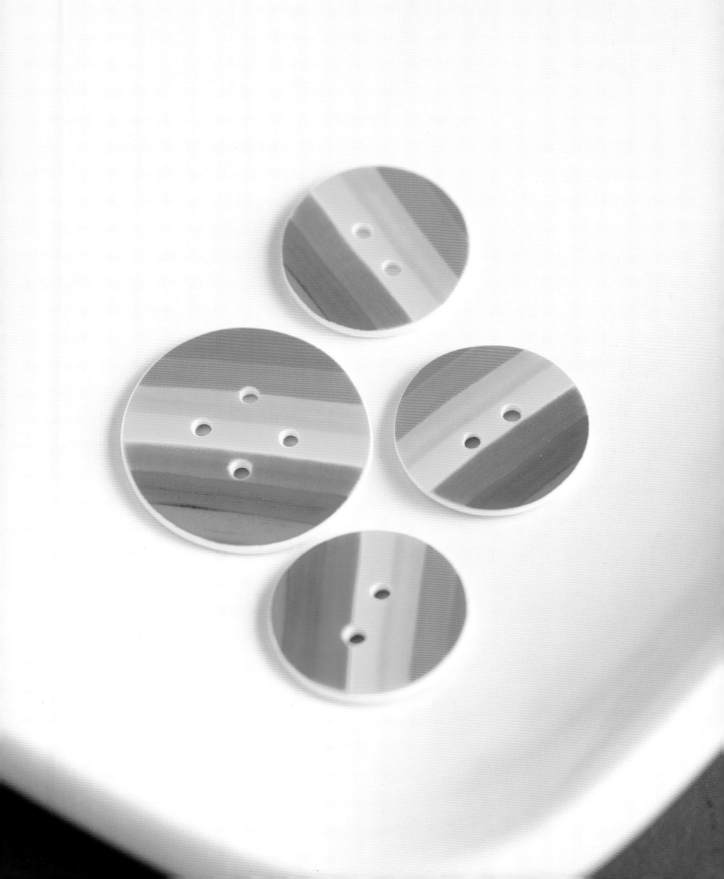

# chevron stripe earrings

*designer* **Erin Inglis**

## what you'll need

- 400-grit sandpaper
- sheet of clear shrink plastic
- template (optional)* (below)
- black ultra-fine point permanent marker
- bullet-tipped art markers in your choice of colors
- scissors
- craft knife
- parchment paper
- gloss spray sealant
- earring findings: four jump rings, two ear hooks
- 2 small pairs of needle-nose pliers

*If you reproduce the template provided at 100%, once shrunk, the earrings will measure approximately ⅞ inches (2.2 cm) long.

## what you do

**1** Thoroughly sand one side of the shrink plastic in an area large enough to fit two earrings.

**2** If you're using the template, transfer it by placing it on a flat surface and setting the shrink plastic on top of it, smooth side up. Trace the black lines using a black marker, and then repeat a second time elsewhere on the plastic for the second earring. If you aren't using the template, draw the outline and design freehand, using the photo as a guide.

**3** Let the outlines dry for a few minutes. Flip the plastic over so the rough side faces up, and color the template in with the art markers.

**4** Cut the earrings out. Use the craft knife to cut the hole for the finding.

**5** Place the plastic rough side down on a piece of parchment paper to prevent sticking and shrink the plastic according to the manufacturer's directions.

**6** When the earrings have shrunk and cooled, sand the edges and cover both sides with several thin coats of spray sealant.

**7** To complete your earrings, attach the findings using the pliers (one pair in each hand) to open and close the jump rings.

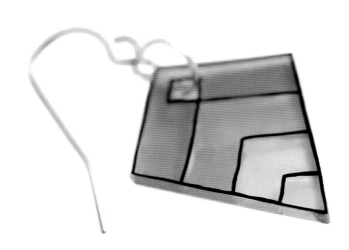

## template

template is actual size

# terra-cotta pot

## designer Erin Inglis

### what you'll need

- roll of masking tape (optional)
- unsealed terra-cotta pot
- water-based paint markers of your choice

**TIP:**

- Consider sealing your pot with a waterproof varnish if you're going to use it outside.

### what you do

1. If you need a guide for the straight lines in the design, apply strips of masking tape to the pot to act as a straight edge. Just be sure you don't place tape on wet paint.

2. Using the photo as a guide, draw your design onto the pot with the water-based markers. I made my design by drawing a row of triangles around the bottom and then working upward.

3. Color in the shapes you drew. You may have to apply several coats, depending on how opaque you want your design to be.

4. Allow the design to dry completely before handling.

For a completely different look, mark a design only on the rim. A pot with a design marked in gold (snowflakes?) would look pretty and festive for the holidays.

# tissue-stamped earrings

designer **Erin Inglis**

## what you'll need

- clear shrink plastic
- 400-grit sandpaper
- tissue paper
- 3 bullet-tipped art markers in colors of your choice
- circle template or circle craft punch; 1¼ inch (3.2 cm)
- parchment paper
- silver metallic permanent marker
- spray sealant
- industrial-strength craft glue
- earring findings: glue-on bails, kidney earring hooks

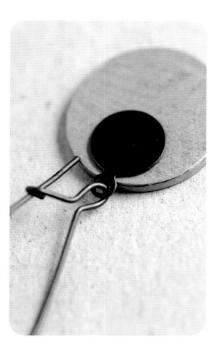

# what you do

1. Sand one side of the shrink plastic. Make the sanded area large enough to fit both earrings.

2. Crumple up the tissue paper into a loose ball.

3. Use one of the markers to color the tissue paper ball on one side like you would to ink a stamp.

4. Stamp the tissue paper ball randomly all over the sanded area of your shrink plastic. Repeat with two more colors.

5. Punch or cut two circles out of the sanded and stamped area.

6. Set the circles on parchment paper to prevent sticking, and then shrink the plastic according to the manufacturer's instructions.

7. When the earrings have shrunk and cooled, sand the edges smooth.

8. Color the edges with silver marker.

9. Apply a thin layer of sealant to the stamped side of the earrings, and once it has dried, color over the stamped colors with the silver marker. Putting a coat of sealant on first prevents the silver marker from making your other colors run. (The side you're coloring on will be the back, and the design will be seen through the clear plastic from the other side.)

10. Coat both sides with several thin layers of sealant. Even though there is no ink on the front of the earring, a coat or two of sealant will help to prevent scratching.

11. Once everything is dry, glue on the bails and attach the kidney hooks. Be sure to orient the findings so that the side you didn't color faces out.

# two-tone post earrings

## designer Erin Inglis

### what you'll need

- white inkjet shrink plastic*
- shape template with squares and circles**
- bullet-tipped art markers: any two colors
- pencil
- scissors
- 320-grit sandpaper
- glossy spray sealant
- ⅛ inch (6 mm) or smaller flat earring posts
- industrial-strength craft glue

*You don't need much. This is a great project to do if you have small scraps of inkjet shrink plastic lying around.

**I used an ¹¹⁄₁₆ inch (18 mm) circle template for the round earrings and a 1-inch (2.5 cm) square. After shrinking, these sizes yielded earrings measuring approximately ¼ (6 mm cm) in diameter and ½ inch (1.3 cm) square.

### what you do

1. Find a piece of shrink plastic that will fit two copies of your shape template, and color half of it using broad, even strokes. Repeat on the other half with your second color.

2. Line up your template on the shrink plastic so that the earring has relatively equal parts of each color. Trace the template with your pencil, and repeat for the other earring.

3. Cut out the shapes, and shrink them according to the shrink plastic directions.

4. Once they've cooled down, sand the edges until they're smooth.

5. Apply several coats of sealant to make your earrings shiny and durable.

6. Glue the posts onto the earrings.

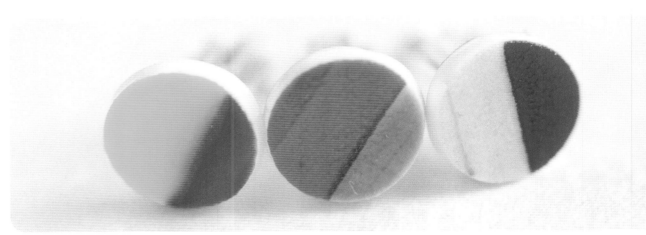

# wooden bangle

### designer **Erin Inglis**

## what you'll need

- measuring tape
- unfinished wood bangle*
- pencil
- water-based neon paint pen
- metallic permanent marker
- glossy spray-on sealant

*found at craft stores and on Etsy

## what you do

**1** Using your measuring tape as a guide, draw a grid with the pencil on your bangle. I used a ¼-inch (6 mm) square grid on the yellow bracelet and a ⅛-inch (3 mm) square grid on the pink one. I'll refer to the ⅛-inch grid in the instructions, but you should use whatever fits best on your bangle.

**2** To start the grid, measure and mark ⅛-inch-wide sections in at least four places around the bangle. Wrap the measuring tape around the bracelet so you can draw straight lines connecting your marks.

**3** Once you have the bangle "striped," make marks in ⅛-inch increments all the way around on each rim edge. Make sure the top marks and bottom marks line up with one another so you can draw vertical lines connecting them.

**4** Connect the top and bottom marks across the width of the bangle, and you should have an even grid.

**5** Use the neon paint pen to color the inside of the bracelet, along with its outer edges. You may need to apply a few coats.

**6** Use the metallic marker to color in random groups of squares all over the grid you've created.

**7** Let the ink and paint dry thoroughly and then erase all the leftover grid lines.

**8** Use the neon paint pen to fill in some of the remaining exposed wood spaces.

**9** When the paint is dry, apply the spray sealant to make the bangle shiny and durable. Use several thin coats on both sides, letting each one dry completely before applying the next.

# upcycled bottles
## designer Esther Coombs

## what you'll need

- empty wine bottle*
- dish soap
- masking tape
- piece of cardboard, at least 20 inches (50.8 cm) square
- small table or a sturdy stool
- white spray paint
- templates, page 104 (optional)
- black permanent marker

*Visit flea markets and garage sales to find old ones with interesting shapes.

## what you do

1 Gather some interesting used bottles.

**TIP:**
- Old medicine bottles work well and are easy to draw on due to their flat sides.

2 Soak the bottles in hot water and dish soap for several hours until the labels slide off. If they won't come off, try scraping them off with a spoon.

3 Dry the bottles thoroughly.

4 Think about your design placement. If you want some areas of the bottle to remain unpainted, then mask off those sections with masking tape.

5 Place the cardboard on a small table or stool, and stand the clean, dry bottles on the cardboard. Putting the bottles on the stool instead of the floor will help to ensure that you spray them evenly. Make sure you're in a well-ventilated space (outside is best, because the fumes are really strong).

6 Follow the instructions on the spray-paint can and apply two coats of paint to the bottle. Try to spray evenly at the recommended distance, or even slightly farther away. You can always move closer, but if you start out too close, you could end up with drips.

7 Once the second coat is dry, peel off any masking tape.

8 Select the template(s) you want to use. Attach the template(s) with a small amount of masking tape.

9 Trace around the edge of the template with the marker. Be careful, though. There are no second chances with a permanent marker on top of spray paint! It's better to keep the outline thin to begin with, as you can always make it thicker or add to the basic lines later.

10 Once you've traced the template(s), have a look at your design and see where you can add additional details. For your first attempt at adding details to your bottle design, why not try drawing windows? Draw four small rectangles close together, two above, two below, and color them in. You'll be surprised by how much this adds to the design.

# templates

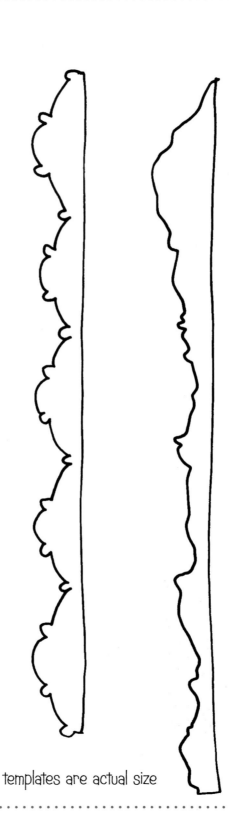

templates are actual size

# teacups and saucers

designer Esther Coombs

## what you'll need

- new or good-condition old teacups and saucers (no chips or cracks in the glaze)
- templates, page 108 (optional)
- scissors
- thick paper for tracing the templates (optional)
- masking tape
- fine-tip ceramic paint marker (or an oil-based paint marker)
- oven

## what you do

**1** Clean the cups and saucers in the dishwasher on a hot cycle or wash them by hand in hot water. There are two reasons to do this: First, they will be very clean. Second, if they survive the dishwasher, then there is a very good chance they will survive the oven bake required to set the design. If the china cracks or chips, or the surface glaze cracks, you'll want to find some different cups to use for the project.

**2** Select a template and trace it onto thick paper, cut it out, and then stick it to the cup with masking tape. Once you have tried this a few times, you might want to design your own templates freehand, or use real doilies to create new designs.

**3** Pump the tip of the ceramic marker on a paper towel or piece of scrap paper to get the paint flowing. If the ink flows too quickly, blot it with your cloth. If it flows too slowly, pump the tip, shake the pen, and pump the tip again. It's important to get the ink to flow steadily before you begin in order to avoid blotches.

**4** Holding the cup or saucer in one hand, and the ceramic marker in the other, trace the edges of the template onto the china. Follow the edges closely without touching them. Don't run under the edges. You want to keep the line steady and even if possible. Practice makes perfect!

**5** Once you've traced all the way around the template, set the cup or saucer aside to dry for 10 minutes, and then peel off the template and masking tape. Feel free at this point to add your own designs and doodles to the basic template shape or repeat the template edge in several positions around the cup. If you find you don't like your design after you remove the template, don't panic! At this point you can wipe it all off with a rag and rubbing alcohol, or tidy up any small mistakes with a cotton swab dipped in rubbing alcohol.

**6** Set your ceramic piece aside for 24 hours to dry completely.

**7** Put the cup in the oven, set the temperature to 300°F (150°C), and bake it at that temperature for 35 minutes. I prefer to let the china warm up slowly, placing it in the oven before turning it on. I think this helps to prevent breaking, chipping, and cracking.

**8** Once the bake is finished, turn the oven off and leave the door slightly ajar to let the china cool slowly. You can easily smear the design when it's wet, so try not to touch the china until it's completely cool.

Don't limit yourself to plain cups and saucers. If you come across a set with a design you love, snap it up! Your doodled art can enhance the existing motif and make it even more interesting.

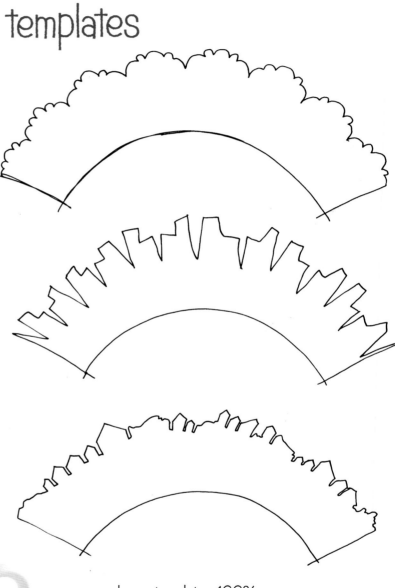

# templates

enlarge templates 100%

# decorated
# chargers

designer Ishtar Olivera Belart

## what you'll need

- plain, large ceramic charger plate
- rubbing alcohol
- ceramic paint markers, in colors of choice
- templates, page 111 (optional)
- toothpick (optional)
- oven

## what you do

1. Clean the plate thoroughly and wipe it down with rubbing alcohol. Make sure it's completely dry before you start.

2. Using the paint markers, begin drawing your design. Draw only around the rim so that you can still see the design when you set a dinner plate on top of the charger. Wipe off any mistakes as you go with a damp cloth or paper towel. Use a little rubbing alcohol for stubborn marks. Cotton swabs are good for wiping away tiny details.

3. Follow the manufacturer's instructions for heat setting the design. I let my plate dry for 24 hours and then baked it in an oven at 325°F (162°C) for 40 minutes.

**TIP:**

● To draw very tiny details like eyes, noses, or flowers, let some of the marker's paint leak out onto a piece of cardboard by pressing down on the tip and holding it there. Pick up the paint with the end of a toothpick and use it as a pencil to draw on the plate. The paint on the cardboard will dry fast, so you'll need to keep pouring fresh paint from time to time.

# templates

enlarge templates 100%

# gift tags

designer Ishtar Olivera Belart

## what you'll need

- adhesive labels OR precut cardboard tags OR tags you cut by hand or using a craft punch

- templates, page 114 (optional)

- 3D or glow-in-the-dark craft pens

- very fine-tipped (0.3) metal-tipped markers in your choice of colors

You can find adhesive-backed labels/paper at most office supply stores. Use a paper punch or decorative-edged scissors to make labels in any shape from the paper. The labels are perfect for gift packages—just peel and stick!

## what you do

1. Draw a design freehand or trace and transfer one of the templates onto a precut or hand-cut label.

2. Color in the design with the fine-tipped markers and set the labels aside to dry.

# templates

To:
From:

templates are actual size

# mandala pebbles

designer **Maria M. Trujillo A. (aka MagaMerlina)**

## what you'll need

- dark-colored pebbles with a smooth, flat surface*
- spray varnish, matte finish (optional)
- white pencil
- waterproof white India Ink
- dip pen with a 512 nib, or a very fine round brush (00 or 000)

*I prefer disc-shaped pebbles. They accommodate a round design, but they're flat enough to draw or paint on.

## what you do

1. Wash the pebbles in soapy water and let them dry.

2. Apply a coat of spray varnish or a sealant and let that dry. This will make the surface smoother to draw on, but it's entirely optional.

3. If you're drawing freehand, start in the center and draw the basic design on the pebble using the white pencil.

4. Using the dip pen or brush, go over the basic design using white ink.

5. Add the details and let it dry.

6. Finish with a coat of spray varnish (optional).

# templates

templates are actual size

# keepsake box

designer Maria M. Trujillo A. (aka MagaMerlina)

## what you'll need

- ¾-inch (1.9 cm) flat paintbrush
- white gesso
- wooden box, sanded
- template, page 119
- 6H pencil
- No. 7 round paintbrush
- acrylic paints in two colors of your choice
- a palette or a plastic dish to mix the acrylic paints
- waterproof white India ink
- a dip pen with a 512 nib, or a very fine round brush (00 or 000)
- spray varnish (optional)

## what you do

**1** Using the flat brush, prime the lid of the box with white gesso. You can prime the whole box if you'd like. Let the gesso dry.

**2** Using the template as a guide, draw the basic shape of the fish and the bigger details using the 6H pencil.

**3** Using the round brush, paint the fish with a mixture of the two acrylic paints, varying it with different shades to make it more interesting. An uneven look is perfect!

**4** When the acrylic paint is completely dry, add all of the white details and mandalas with the white ink, using the dip pen or the very fine brush.

**5** If desired, when the box is dry, apply a varnish to seal it.

# template

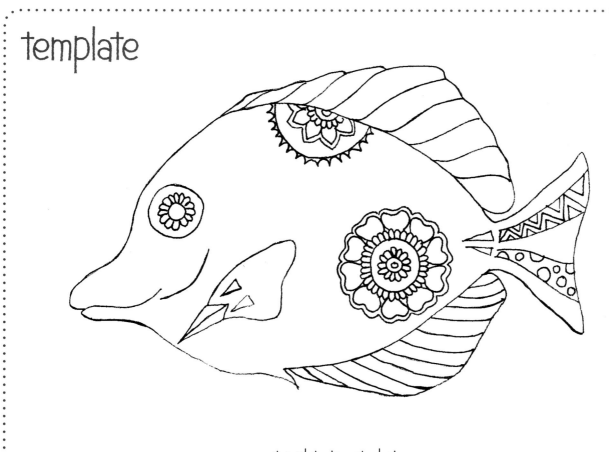

template is actual size

# wooden eggs

designer **Maria M. Trujillo A. (aka MagaMerlina)**

## what you'll need

- wooden eggs
- 6H pencil*
- templates, below (optional)
- pigmented India-ink artist pens with brush nibs in your choice of colors
- black waterproof fine liner (0.25 or 0.3 tip)

\* I recommended the 6H pencil because it makes very light lines that won't show through your final design.

## what you do

1. On the wider end of the egg, draw a basic design using the 6H pencil. If desired, use the templates. Draw the shaded part of the design first and then add the rest.

2. Starting in the center of the design, color all of the shapes using the brush pens. Let the egg dry completely. (*Note:* The India ink in the brush pens is waterproof and permanent.)

3. Using the black pen, outline all of the shapes and add the details.

4. Sign and date the other end of your egg. Let it dry.

## templates

templates are actual size

# stacking bowl trio

designer **Lena Hanzel**

## what you'll need

- black fine-tip ceramic/porcelain marker
- white porcelain bowl/s*
- templates, page 125 (optional)

* if you use vintage dishes, make sure that the porcelain has no visible hairline cracks. The paint could run into those cracks and ruin your pattern.

## what you do

**1** Test the marker on the bowl in an inconspicuous place. Draw the first lines of your pattern directly onto the bowl. Try to avoid touching the areas you're planning to paint. If you leave fingerprints, wipe them away before moving on.

**TIP:**

- Wherever you stop drawing and lift the marker, a thick color application that resembles a dot will appear. For this reason, I try to strategically plan my drawing so that a line ends where a dot will later be drawn.

**2** When you've gone nearly all the way around the bowl, stop drawing. Wait 10-15 minutes for the paint to dry.

**3** Finish the lines, let the bowl dry for another 10-15 minutes, and then add the dots.

**4** Once you've completed the pattern, let the bowl dry for 24 hours.

**5** Follow the manufacturer's instructions for baking the piece. I baked mine for 90 minutes at 320°F (160°C). I didn't preheat the oven; I put the bowl in and let it warm up gradually. After 90 minutes, I turned the heat off and left the bowl in the oven to cool down.

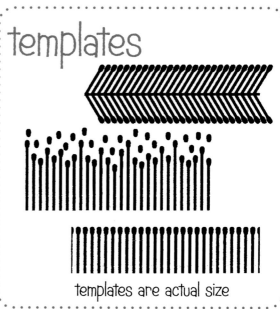

templates

templates are actual size

# about the designers

**Fusun Aydinlik** is a Turkish artist. After working as a television producer in Istanbul for several years, she simplified her life by relocating to a small town in the North Aegean, a move that allowed her to raise her young son more naturally and spend more time on her arts and crafts. Fusun studied industrial engineering and worked in the film business for many years. She is now teaching herself to draw, paint, and collage. Her work is sold in Turkey and online. To learn more about Fusun, go to www.facebook.com/zeustones or www. etsy.com/shop/zeustones.

**Ishtar Olivera Belart** is a children's illustrator from Spain whose passion for art began at an early age. Her work is influenced by her many travels around the world and by childhood years spent in Mexico. Japanese-inspired themes and aesthetics, both traditional and contemporary, also feature prominently in her work. These cultural influences, together with Ishtar's love for color, nature, and the simple things in life, make for a unique and signature style in her illustrations and crafts. Ishtar lives in England where she teaches craft workshops and works as a freelance artist.

An artist based in Hampshire, England, **Esther Coombs** believes that life is a story, and that narrative is best told with drawings. In a garden shed behind her house, she creates up-cycled vintage ceramics and other art, all featuring her hand-drawn illustrations. Esther's goal is to bring new layers of narrative to each carefully constructed piece. She loves to give discarded items new life. With the aid of her young daughter and two cats, Esther works mainly on commissioned illustrations and a few small personal pieces. To see more of Esther's art, check out her website, www.esthercoombs.com. To purchase her work, go to www.esthercoombs.etsy.com.

Originally from Taipei, Taiwan, **Flora Chang** holds an M.F.A. from the Academy of Art University in San Francisco. She joined Hallmark Cards 13 years ago and has been a full-time designer ever since, creating and illustrating products for kids. In 2007, she started her blog, Happy Doodle Land, as a creative endeavor outside of work. Her favorite activity is drawing—she's never without a sketchbook and a black marker. Flora also loves making things with her hands, taking classes to learn new skills, going on road trips, and treasure-hunting at flea markets. She's most inspired by folk art, vintage children's illustrations, and organic shapes, colors, and textures. Her website is www. HappyDoodleLand.com. Visit her Etsy shop at www.etsy.com/ shop/HappyDoodleLand.

**April Deacon** is a painter and mixed-media artist. Through her work, she reinvents artifacts from the past and celebrates the present. April holds a B.F.A. from Ohio Wesleyan University and an M.A. from Marshall University. A high-school art teacher since 2003, she lives in southern Ohio with her husband, Michael, and their two daughters, Gabrielle and Olivia, who keep her inspired. To see April's complete portfolio, go to www.aprildeacon.com. You can purchase her original work at www.etsy.com/shop/ aprilawakening.

A mother and freelance illustrator/designer living in sunny Indonesia, **Ning Fathia** describes herself as an occasional crafter. She loves all colors equally. Ning spends her free time playing with her daughter and drawing. She maintains her blog, www.babalisme. blogspot.com, as a creative outlet where she can express her gratitude to the craft community for its inspiration.

A resident of Ontario, Canada, where she grew up, **Amber Gameiro** has been crafting for as long as she can remember. She now considers it an obsession instead of a hobby. Her favorite media include yarn, felt, paint, and reused items. She believes in simplicity, accessibility, and sharing when it comes to crafts and creative ideas. In 2011, this belief led Amber to start SaltTree, an online forum for sharing recipes, crafts, and DIY-project tutorials. As a wife and mother, Amber finds inspiration for new projects in family moments and life's adventures. Visit her at www.salttree.net or www.etsy.com/shop/SaltTree

**Lena Hanzel** is a graphic designer based in Berlin, Germany. In 2012, after working for several agencies as a freelancer, she started her own company and website, There Is Always Room for Emptiness. Lena now produces her own line of products, including hand-painted dishware and tea towels, that combine her passion for drawing with her love for vintage items. To see more of her work, visit roomforemptiness.etsy.com or check out her blog: room-for-emptiness.com.

**Abbey Hendrickson** is an artist and blogger who lives in Owego, New York, with her husband and two children. She earned a B.F.A. from SUNY Brockport in 2004 and an M.F.A. in visual studies from the University at Buffalo in 2009. Abbey writes a daily lifestyle blog called Aesthetic Outburst (www.aestheticoutburst.blogspot.com), where she chronicles the adventures of her family as well as the ongoing renovation of their nineteenth-century farmhouse. Her work can be found in *Drawn In: A Peek into the Inspiring Sketchbooks of 44 Fine Artists, Illustrators, Graphic Designers, and Cartoonists* by Julia Rothman; *State of Craft* by Victoria Woodcock and Cigalle Hanaor; and *Old School: Art Inspired by the Aesthetics of 20th Century Education* by Janine Vangool. Hendrickson has been a guest contributor on several popular blogs, including sfgirlbybay, Poppytalk, and A Beautiful Mess. She's the author of the book *You Are Awesome: 21 Crafts to Make You Happy*, which was published by Cicada Books in 2012.

**Erin Inglis** resides in the beautiful backwoods of Vermont, where she spends most of her time adding bright colors to anything she can get her hands on and forgetting to water her plants. You can find her artwork, jewelry, blog, and more at ErinInglis.com.

Known for her bold, folksy floral patterns, **Dinara Mirtalipova** is an Uzbek artist and children's book illustrator. Dinara graduated from the University of Economics in Tashkent, Uzbekistan, with a major in cybernetics. She discovered her passion for drawing shortly after finishing school and decided to pursue a career in art. Now a mother of one, Dinara currently focuses on designs and drawings for children. She finds inspiration in folk music, myths, and fairy tales.

**Dora Moreland** has been crafting for as long as she can remember. She grew up in Hungary, a country that values folk arts and crafts, surrounded by her mother's creations. Although she has lived in the United States for many years, Dora considers herself a Hungarian and is strongly influenced by her heritage. A stay-at-home mom to five children who volunteers as a Cub-Scout leader and manages to cook dinner on an almost-daily basis, Dora loves to read, craft, sew, knit, and make jewelry. She secretly wishes she could invent a contraption that would harvest and bottle her sons' unlimited energy. In her spare time, Dora blogs at www.untrendylife.com. Check out her Etsy store: PaulStreetShop.

**Maria M. Trujillo A. (aka MagaMerlina)** is a self-proclaimed late-blooming artist-crafter from Bogotá, Colombia, who now calls New Zealand (Land of the Long White Cloud) home. Maria attended medical school and has worked as a psychiatrist. When she moved to New Zealand in 2008, she was inspired to try her hand at arts and crafts. She began with embroidery and discovered that it offered endless possibilities. Color became her passion, and she worked for a long time from other people's designs before creating her own. She taught herself to draw and has tried almost every medium available, though watercolor and ink are her favorites. Mandalas have long been a theme in her arts and crafts. Visit Maria at www.magamerlina.com.

# index

# acknowledgments

A standing ovation to all the incredibly talented designers who contributed their time and creativity to this book. You ladies are terrific!

# credits

Editor: Linda Kopp

Art Director: Carol Barnao

Cover Designer: Kristi Pfeffer

Photographer: Lynne Harty